INVASION ALERT!

INVASION OF THE BULLFROGS

Enslow PUBLISHING

DEVON PATRICK

Please visit our website, www.enslow.com. For a free color catalog of all our high-quality books, call toll free 1-800-398-2504 or fax 1-877-980-4454

Published in 2027 by
Enslow Publishing
2544 Clinton Street
Buffalo, NY 14224

Portions of this work were originally authored by Therese Shea and published as *Animal Invaders: Destroying Native Habitats: Attack of the Bullfrogs*. All new material in this edition is authored by Devon Patrick.

Cataloging-in-Publication Data
Names: Patrick, Devon.
Title: Invasion of the bullfrogs / Devon Patrick.
Description: Buffalo, NY : Enslow Publishing, 2027. | Series: Invasion alert! | Includes glossary and index.
Identifiers: ISBN 9781978548336 (pbk.) | ISBN 9781978548343 (library bound) | ISBN 9781978548350 (ebook)
Subjects: LCSH: Bullfrog--Control--Juvenile literature. | Introduced amphibians--Juvenile literature. | Invasive species--Control--Juvenile literature.
Classification: LCC QL668.E27 D486 2027 | DDC 597.892--dc23

Printed in China

Photos Credits: Cover, p. 1 Jennifer-Davis/Shutterstock.com; cover, p. 1, 3, 4, 6, 8, 10, 12, 14, 16, 18, 20, 22, 23, 24 (dot pattern) Nurin Nabila A/Shutterstock.com; p. 4, 6, 8, 10, 12, 14, 16, 18, 20 (sidebar frame) HST6/Shutterstock.com; p. 5 Wirestock Creators/Shutterstock.com; p. 7 H M Thompson/Shutterstock.com; p. 9 Lawrence Lee Derge/Shutterstock.com; p. 10 Paul S. Wolf/Shutterstock.com; p. 11 Gordon Magee/Shutterstock.com; p. 15 Milan Zygmunt/Shutterstock.com; p. 17 wasin suriyawan/Shutterstock.com; p. 19 Eivor Kuchta/Shutterstock.com; p. 20 Lensa Images/Shutterstock.com; p. 21 USGS Arizona Cooperative Fish and Wildlife Research Unit

CPSIA compliance information: Batch #QSENS27: For further information, contact Enslow Publishing, New York, New York, at 1-800-398-2504.

CONTENTS

Words in the glossary appear in **bold** type the first time they are used in the text.

WHAT'S THAT NOISE?

A deep call erupts over the wetlands. What could be making such a loud sound? It might be a bullfrog!

Bullfrogs have a deep call, or croak, that can be heard a half mile (0.8 km) away. It can be as loud as a jet taking off or a motorcycle cruising down the highway. Some people think the bullfrog's croak sounds like the noise a bull makes—that's how the frog got its name!

Bullfrogs are not poisonous. But in certain parts of the world, that loud croak can mean big trouble.

STAY ALERT

A bullfrog's croak sounds like it's saying *jug-o-rum* or *rum-hum*.

Only male bullfrogs croak. They do this to attract **mates**.

MEET THE BULLFROG

The American bullfrog is the largest frog in North America. It can weigh as much as 1.5 pounds (0.7 kg).

A bullfrog's body is about 8 inches (20 cm) long. It has powerful back legs that can be 10 inches (25 cm) long. It can jump as far as 6 feet (1.8 m)!

The American bullfrog is native to the central and eastern United States and southeastern Canada. Like all frogs, bullfrogs are amphibians. They need to live in or near fresh water. Bullfrogs like warm, calm, shallow waters, such as ponds and lakes.

STAY ALERT

It's easy to tell male and female bullfrogs apart. Females are larger.

Bullfrogs are usually green or brown with a white or yellow underside. This coloring allows them to blend in with their surroundings and hide from predators.

BULLFROGS ARE BORN

Mating season takes place from May to July in northern areas and from February to October in southern areas.

The female bullfrog lays her eggs in water. She may lay up to 20,000 eggs at once! The male bullfrog then **fertilizes** them. The eggs float on the water's surface.

Soon, a **tadpole hatches** from the egg. Bullfrog tadpoles live in water. They are dark green or black in color. Over time, the tadpoles grow legs and lose their tail. It may take as long as four years, but finally, the tadpoles come out of the water as adult bullfrogs. After about two more years, the bullfrogs are old enough to mate.

STAY ALERT

During mating season, male bullfrogs may have a yellow throat. Females have white throats.

Bullfrog tadpoles grow to be about 6 inches (15 cm) long.

GROWING POPULATIONS

The number of bullfrogs is growing quickly, especially compared to other frog species.

Bullfrogs lay many more eggs than other kinds of North American frogs. Many of these frogs' eggs and tadpoles are eaten before they become adults, but bullfrog eggs and tadpoles are more likely to survive. This is because they don't taste good to many fish!

Bullfrogs do have some predators, including herons, turtles, water snakes, raccoons, and even people. Frog legs are eaten by people around the world. They are considered a **delicacy** in France!

This great blue heron caught a bullfrog for its midday snack.

MOVING IN

While the American bullfrog is native to the eastern United States, it has spread across the country. Some of the spread was by accident. People may have accidentally picked up bullfrog eggs when they've taken water from one source to fill other ponds and lakes.

In other places, people introduced bullfrogs on purpose. People brought bullfrogs to California in the 1890s so they could eat frog legs! Other people brought bullfrogs to new places as pets. Sometimes, when these pet bullfrogs grew too big for their indoor aquariums, they were released into the wild.

Bullfrogs spread naturally too. They like to live alone and have their own territory. They can easily hop from one water source to another and may choose to do so if their home gets too crowded.

STAY ALERT

Now, bullfrogs can even be found in some parts of California's deserts!

BULLFROG RANGE
Canada
United States
Mexico
WA
MT
ND
MN
OR
ID
SD
WY
WI
MI
NY
VT
ME
NH
MA
RI
CT
PA
NJ
DE
MD
IA
NE
IL
IN
OH
WV
VA
NV
UT
CO
KS
MO
KY
NC
CA
TN
SC
AZ
NM
OK
AR
MS
AL
GA
LA
TX
FL
native bullfrogs
nonnative bullfrogs
Bullfrogs now live around the world. They can be found in Mexico, Cuba, Europe, South America, and Asia!

UNWELCOME GUESTS

Bullfrogs can harm **habitats** where they don't belong. They are an **invasive species**. They compete with other animals for food, and usually win! This leaves less food than usual for the species that normally live there. Less food means more stress for those animals, so they may not reproduce as much.

Bullfrogs have big appetites. They will eat nearly anything, including snakes, worms, bugs, eggs, mice, birds, and other frogs—even other bullfrogs! If an animal fits in a bullfrog's mouth, it's dinner. They may even eat **endangered** species!

STAY ALERT

Bullfrogs are nocturnal. They hunt at night. When something tasty comes by, they jump on it.

This bullfrog gets ready to munch on a grasshopper.

A DEADLY FUNGUS

Frogs all over the world can die from the chytrid (KY-truhd) **fungus**. It causes a skin **disease** that can kill amphibians in just weeks. **Infected** animals spread the fungus when they're set free in the wild or when water they've used is dumped into a lake or pond.

The bullfrog trade plays a part in the fungus's spread. Each year, more than 2 million bullfrogs are imported into California. These bullfrogs are typically used for food, as pets, or for dissection in classrooms. However, many of them carry the fungus. When infected frogs are moved from place to place, the deadly fungus travels with them.

STAY ALERT

Bullfrogs at stores in several U.S. cities were tested for the chytrid fungus. About 40 percent were infected.

The chytrid fungus has caused the number of amphibians to decrease around the world.

TAKING ACTION

People are beginning to take action against bullfrogs in nonnative habitats.

Governments in many areas of the United States and Canada are allowing people to hunt bullfrogs. They're also introducing animals that are known to eat bullfrogs, such as largemouth bass, into the habitats. Some places have laws that make it illegal to sell, move, or keep bullfrogs.

Still, bullfrogs are very hard to control. Bullfrogs don't have many natural predators in nonnative habitats, which makes it hard to keep their population in check.

STAY ALERT

The chytrid fungus may have caused about 100 frog species to become extinct, or die out.

Bullfrogs can easily hop from one water source to another. They can adapt and survive in many different environments, which makes them difficult to control.

STOP THOSE FROGS!

Amphibian populations are in danger. Studies show that about 40 percent of amphibian species are in danger of dying out. This is mostly because of climate change, habitat destruction, pollution, and the chytrid fungus. But hungry bullfrogs can make things worse when they're introduced into places where they shouldn't be!

You can help with the fight against invasive bullfrogs. Don't buy bullfrogs or bullfrog tadpoles from stores. Don't keep them as pets. And spread the word to neighbors who might buy bullfrogs for backyard ponds.

Just remember—bullfrogs aren't all bad. They just need to stay where they're supposed to!

Bullfrogs can be dangerous when they're outside their native habitats. But there are ways you can help!

GLOSSARY

delicacy: something pleasing to eat that is considered rare or luxurious

disease: an illness that affects a person, animal, or plant

endangered: in danger of dying out

fertilizes: to add male cells to a female's eggs to make babies

fungus: a growing thing that may resemble a plant but lacks green color and cannot make its own food, instead living on or in plants, animals, or dying matter

habitats: the natural place where an animal or plant lives

hatches: to break open or come out of

infected: to cause someone or something to become sick or affected by disease

invasive species: one kind of living thing likely to spread and be harmful when placed in a new area

mate: one of two animals that come together to make babies

tadpole: the larva of an amphibian, such as a frog or toad

FACT CHECK

1. Bullfrogs are________ .
   a. reptiles b. amphibians c. mammals

2. How many eggs can female bullfrogs lay at one time?
   a. 1,000 b. 10,000 c. 20,000

3. Bullfrogs are native to________ .
   a. the eastern U.S. b. the western U.S. c. Asia

Answers: 1. b, 2. c, 3. a

ON THE INTERNET

American Bullfrog

www.nationalgeographic.com/animals/amphibians/facts/american-bullfrog

Wondering what the bullfrog sounds like? Hear it here!

American Bullfrog

www.biokids.umich.edu/critters/Lithobates_catesbeianus/

Discover more information about the bullfrog's life cycle.

Publisher's note to educators and parents: Our editors have carefully reviewed these websites to ensure that they are suitable for students. Many websites change frequently, however, and we cannot guarantee that a site's future contents will continue to meet our high standards of quality and educational value. Be advised that students should be closely supervised whenever they access the Internet.

INDEX